# Classy Trash Bags & Accessories™

## General Information

Many of the products used in this pattern book can be purchased from local craft, fabric and variety stores, or from the Annie's Attic Needlecraft Catalog (see Customer Service information on page 15).

## General Instructions

The designs are made using white plastic kitchen garbage bags, black plastic heavy duty lawn and garden bags or recycled plastic shopping bags.

To make strips, lay the bag out flat. Cut off the top of the bag if it has handles or a drawstring. Cut seam off bottom of bag.

Measure and cut the remainder of the bag into 2-inch strips. Each strip will form a circle. Do not cut, leave as a circle.

Lay the cut circles out flat in strips, and tie one to the next until all the circles are tied together, forming 1 long, double-layered strip.

Continue this process until you reach your desired length. The number of bags needed varies according to the estimated amounts called for in each pattern. ■

# Vintage Beads Bag

## SKILL LEVEL

EASY

## FINISHED SIZE

6 inches deep x 8 inches wide, not including Strap

## MATERIALS

- Plastic shopping bags: Approximately 12 desired color
- Plastic lawn and garden bags: 3 black
- Size K/10½/6.5mm crochet hook or size needed to obtain gauge
- Tapestry needle
- Black sewing thread
- Black trim with dangle beads: 21 inches
- Embellishments of choice
- Craft glue or hot glue gun
- Stitch marker

## GAUGE

3 sc = 1 inch; 3 sc rows = 1 inch

## PATTERN NOTES

Read General Instructions before beginning pattern.

Do not join or turn rounds unless otherwise stated. Mark first stitch of each round.

## INSTRUCTIONS

### BAG

**Rnd 1:** With shopping bag strip, ch 14, 3 sc in 2nd ch from hook, sc in each of next 11 chs, 3 sc in last ch, working on opposite side of starting ch, sc in each of next 11 chs. *(28 sc)*

**Rnd 2:** 2 sc in each of first 3 sts, sc in each of next 11 sts, 2 sc in each of next 3 sts, sc in each of last 11 sts, join in beg sc. *(34 sc)*

**Rnd 3:** *[2 sc in next st, sc in next st] 3 times, sc in each of next 11 sts, rep from * once. *(40 sc)*

**Rnd 4:** *[2 sc in next st, sc in each of next 2 sts] 3 times, sc in each of next 11 sts, rep from * once. *(46 sc)*

**Rnd 5:** [Sc in each of next 3 sts, 2 sc in next st] 3 times, sc in each of next 14 sts, [2 sc in next st, sc in each of next 3 sts] 3 times, sc in each of last 8 sts. *(52 sc)*

**Rnd 6:** Working this rnd in **back lps** *(see Stitch Guide)* only, sc in each st around.

**Rnds 7–20:** Sc in each st around.

**Rnd 21:** Sc in each st around, join with sl st in beg sc. Fasten off.

**Rnd 22:** Join lawn bag strip with sc in first st, sc in each st around.

**Rnd 23:** Ch 1, sc in each st around, join with sl st in beg sc. Fasten off.

**Rnd 24:** For **trim**, with bottom of Bag facing, working in rem lps of rnd 5, join lawn bag strip with sc in first st, sc in each st around, join with sl st in beg sc. Fasten off.

Glue beaded trim to rnd 22 with beads at bottom *(see photo)*.

**STRAP**

**Row 1:** With lawn bag strip, ch 5, sc in 2nd ch from hook and in each ch across, turn. *(4 sc)*

**Row 2:** Ch 1, sc in each st across, turn.

**Next rows:** Rep row 2 to desired length. Fasten off at end of last row.

Sew 1 end of Strap to each side of Bag.

Embellish as desired. ■

# Crescent Moon Purse

## SKILL LEVEL

EASY

## FINISHED SIZE

12½ inches across

## MATERIALS

- Plastic lawn and garden bags: Approximately 6 black
- Medium (worsted) weight yarn: 25 yds red
- Size K/10½/6.5mm crochet hook or size needed to obtain gauge
- Tapestry needle
- Black sewing thread
- Black arched plastic purse handles: 5½ inches across
- Embellishments of choice
- Stitch marker

## GAUGE

5 sc = 2 inches; 5 sc rows = 2 inches

## PATTERN NOTES

Read General Instructions before beginning pattern.

Do not join or turn rounds unless otherwise stated. Mark first stitch of each round.

## INSTRUCTIONS

### PURSE

**Rnd 1:** With black strip, ch 6, 3 sc in 2nd ch from hook, sc in each of next 3 chs, 3 sc in last ch, working on opposite side of ch, sc in each of next 3 chs. *(12 sc)*

**Rnd 2:** [Sc in next st, 2 sc in next st] around. *(18 sc)*

**Rnds 3 & 4:** [2 sc in next st, sc in each of next 2 sts] around. *(24 sc, 32 sc)*

**Rnd 5:** [Sc in each of next 3 sts, 2 sc in next st] around. *(40 sc)*

**Rnd 6:** [2 sc in next st, sc in each of next 4 sts] around. *(48 sc)*

**Rnd 7:** [Sc in each of next 5 sts, 2 sc in next st] around. *(56 sc)*

**Rnd 8:** [2 sc in next st, sc in each of next 6 sts] around. *(64 sc)*

**Rnd 9:** [Sc in each of next 7 sts, 2 sc in next st] around. *(72 sc)*

**Rnd 10:** [2 sc in next st, sc in each of next 8 sts] around. *(80 sc)*

**Rnd 11:** [Sc in each of next 9 sts, 2 sc in next st] around. *(88 sc)*

**Rnd 12:** [2 sc in next st, sc in each of next 10 sts] around. *(96 sc)*

**Rnd 13:** [Sc in each of next 11 sts, 2 sc in next st] around. *(104 sc)*

**Rnd 14:** Sc in each st around, join with sl st in beg sc. Fasten off.

**Rnds 15–22:** Sc in each st around.

**Rnd 23:** Sc in each st around, join with sl st in beg sc. Fasten off.

Fold in half lengthwise. Matching rows, sew 14 rows on each side closed, leaving 24 rows at center unsewn.

### TRIM

**Rnd 1:** Working around top opening, join red with sc in any st on 1 side, sc in each st around. *(48 sc)*

**Rnd 2:** Sc in each st around.

**Rnd 3:** Sc in each st around, join with sl st in beg sc. Fasten off. Sew 1 handle to each side of Trim.

Embellish as desired. ■

# WATER BOTTLE

## SKILL LEVEL

EASY

## FINISHED SIZE

3½ inches in diameter x 7½ inches tall, not including Strap

## MATERIALS

- Plastic shopping bags: Approximately 10 white
- Size K/10½/6.5mm crochet hook or size needed to obtain gauge
- Tapestry needle
- Sewing needle
- 1-inch red button
- Embellishments of choice
- Black sewing thread
- Stitch marker

## GAUGE

3 sc = 1 inch; 3 sc rnds = 1 inch

## PATTERN NOTES

Read General Instructions before beginning pattern.

Do not join or turn rounds unless otherwise stated. Mark first stitch of each round.

## INSTRUCTIONS

### COVER

**Rnd 1:** Ch 6, sl st in first ch to form ring, ch 1, 6 sc in ring. *(6 sc)*

**Rnd 2:** 2 sc in each st around. *(12 sc)*

**Rnd 3:** [Sc in next st, 2 sc in next st] around. *(18 sc)*

**Rnd 4:** [Sc in next st, 2 sc in each of next 2 sts] around. *(30 sc)*

**Rnd 5:** Working this rnd in **back lps** *(see Stitch Guide) only,* sc in each st around.

**Rnds 6–25:** Sc in each st around.

**Rnd 26:** Sc in each st around, join with sl st in beg sc. Fasten off.

### STRAP

**Row 1:** Ch 4, sc in 2nd ch from hook and in each ch across, turn. *(3 sc)*

**Row 2:** Ch 1, sc in each st across, turn.

**Next rows:** Rep row 2 to desired length. Fasten off at end of last row.

Sew 1 end of Strap to each side of Cover.

### BUTTONHOLE STRAP

Ch 18. Fasten off.

Sew ends of Strap to back of Cover centered between Strap ends 1½ inches apart.

Sew button to Front of Cover on row 23. Pull Strap to front and loop over button.

Embellish as desired. ■

# Fancy Flower Purse

## SKILL LEVEL

EASY

## FINISHED SIZE

5½ inches deep x 6 inches wide, not including Strap

## MATERIALS

- Plastic lawn and garden bags: Approximately 12 black
- Size K/10½/6.5mm crochet hook or size needed to obtain gauge
- Tapestry needle
- Black sewing thread
- 1-inch button
- Embellishments of choice
- Craft glue or hot glue gun
- Stitch marker

## GAUGE

3 sc = 1 inch; 3 sc rows = 1 inch

## PATTERN NOTES

Read General Instructions before beginning pattern.

Do not join or turn rounds unless otherwise stated. Mark first stitch of each round.

## INSTRUCTIONS

### PURSE

**Rnd 1:** Ch 2, 6 sc in 2nd ch from hook. *(6 sc)*

**Rnd 2:** 2 sc in each st around. *(12 sc)*

**Rnd 3:** [2 sc in next st, sc in next st] around. *(18 sc)*

**Rnd 4:** [2 sc in next st, sc in each of next 2 sts] around. *(24 sc)*

**Rnd 5:** [Sc in each of next 3 sts, 2 sc in next st] around. *(30 sc)*

**Rnd 6:** [2 sc in next st, sc in each of next 4 sts] around. *(36 sc)*

**Rnd 7:** [Sc in each of next 5 sts, 2 sc in next st] around. *(42 sc)*

**Rnd 8:** [2 sc in next st, sc in each of next 6 sts] around. *(48 sc)*

**Rnd 9:** Working this rnd in **back lps** *(see Stitch Guide) only*, sc in each st around.

**Rnds 10–22:** Sc in each st around.

**Rnd 23:** Sc in each st around, join with sl st in beg sc. Fasten off.

**BUTTONHOLE TAB**

**Row 1:** Ch 5, sc in 2nd ch from hook and in each ch across, turn. *(4 sc)*

**Rows 2–9:** Ch 1, sc in each st across, turn.

**Row 10:** Ch 1, sc in first st, for **buttonhole**, ch 3, sk next 2 sts, sc in last st, turn. *(2 sc, 1 ch sp)*

**Row 11:** Ch 1, sc in first st, 3 sc in next ch sp, sc in last st. Fasten off.

Sew row 1 of Tab to row 23 of Purse for center back.

Pull Buttonhole Tab over to front side of Bag and sew button to Bag corresponding with buttonhole.

**STRAP**

**Row 1:** Ch 5, sc in 2nd ch from hook and in each ch across, turn. *(4 sc)*

**Row 2:** Ch 1, sc in each st across, turn.

**Next rows:** Rep row 2 to desired length. Fasten off at end of last row.

Sew 1 end of Strap to each side of Bag.

Embellish Bag as desired. ■

# Pearls & Feathers Bag

**SKILL LEVEL**

**FINISHED SIZE**

6 inches deep x 10 inches wide, not including Strap

**MATERIALS**

- Plastic lawn and garden bags:
  - Approximately 10 black
  - Approximately 3 white
- Size K/10½/6.5mm crochet hook or size needed to obtain gauge
- Tapestry needle
- Black sewing thread
- 4mm pre-strung beads: 1 yd
- Trim:
  - 24 inches black
  - 24 inches white
- 4-inch white silk rose
- Black feathers: 8
- Craft glue or hot glue gun
- Stitch marker

## GAUGE
3 sc = 1 inch; 3 sc rows = 1 inch

## PATTERN NOTES
Read General Instructions before beginning pattern.

Do not join or turn rounds unless otherwise stated. Mark first stitch of each round.

## INSTRUCTIONS

### BAG
**Rnd 1:** With black strip, ch 15, 3 sc in 2nd ch from hook, sc in each of next 12 chs, 3 sc in last ch, working on opposite side of starting ch, sc in each of next 12 chs. *(30 sc)*

**Rnd 2:** 2 sc in each of first 3 sts, sc in each of next 12 sts, 2 sc in each of next 3 sts, sc in each of last 12 sts. *(36 sc)*

**Rnd 3:** *[2 sc in next st, sc in next st] 3 times, sc in each of next 12 sts, rep from * once. *(42 sc)*

**Rnd 4:** [Sc in each of next 2 sts, 2 sc in next st] 3 times, sc in each of next 14 sts, [2 sc in next st, sc in each of next 2 sts] 3 times, sc in each of last 10 sts. *(48 sc)*

**Rnd 5:** *[2 sc in next st, sc in each of next 3 sts] 3 times, sc in each of next 12 sts, rep from * once. *(54 sc)*

**Rnd 6:** Working this rnd in **back lps** *(see Stitch Guide) only,* sc in each st around.

**Rnds 7–16:** Sc in each st around.

**Rnd 17:** Sc in each st around, join with sl st in beg sc. Fasten off.

**Rnd 18:** Join white strip with sc in first st, sc in each st around.

**Rnds 19 & 20:** Sc in each st around.

**Rnd 21:** Sc in each st around, join with sl st in beg sc. Fasten off.

**Rnd 22:** Join black strip with sc in first st, sc in each st around.

**Rnd 23:** Sc in each st around, join with sl st in beg sc. Fasten off.

### STRAP
**Row 1:** With black strip, ch 5, sc in 2nd ch from hook and in each ch across, turn. *(4 sc)*

**Row 2:** Ch 1, sc in each st across, turn.

**Next rows:** Rep row 2 to desired length. Fasten off at end of last row.

Sew 1 end of Strap to each side of Bag.

### FINISHING
1. Glue black trim around Bag over rnd 16.

2. Weave white trim under and over rem lps of sts on rnd 5 *(see photo)* of Bag, secure.

3. Weave pre-strung beads under and over every other st on rnd 23 of Bag, secure.

4. Glue rose to 1 side of Bag for front.

5. Glue ends of Feathers to Bag around sides and bottom of flower *(see photo).* ■

# Summer Clutch

## SKILL LEVEL

EASY

## FINISHED SIZE

6 inches deep x 8½ inches wide

## MATERIALS

- Plastic shopping bags: Approximately 8 white
- Size K/10½/6.5mm crochet hook or size needed to obtain gauge
- Tapestry needle
- 1-inch red button
- Embellishments of choice

## GAUGE

5 sc = 2 inches; 3 sc rows = 1 inch

## PATTERN NOTE

Read General Instructions before beginning pattern.

## INSTRUCTIONS

### BAG

**Row 1:** Ch 33, sc in 2nd ch from hook and in each ch across, turn. *(32 sc)*

**Rows 2–21:** Ch 1, sc in each st across, turn. Fasten off at end of last row.

### FLAP

**Row 1:** Working in ends of row on 1 side of Bag, join with sc in end of first row, sc in each row across, turn. *(21 sc)*

**Rows 2–9:** Ch 1, sc in each st across, turn. Fasten off at end of last row.

## FINISHING

1. Fold up bottom of Bag to top of Bag below Flap, sew side seams.

2. Working in ends of rows on Flap, starting on right-hand side, join with sc in first row, sc in each row across, working in sts across last row, 3 sc in first st, sc in each of next 9 sts, for **buttonhole**, ch 5, sk next st, sc in each of next 9 sts, 3 sc in last st, working in ends of rows, sc in each row across. Fasten off.

3. Join with sc in buttonhole, 4 sc in same sp, sl st in next st on Flap. Fasten off.

4. Fold Flap down over front of Bag and sew button to Bag corresponding to buttonhole.

5. Embellish as desired. ■

# Black Rose **Bag**

## SKILL LEVEL

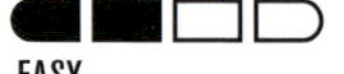


## FINISHED SIZE

6 inches deep x 8 inches wide, not including Strap

## MATERIALS

- Plastic shopping bags: Approximately 18 desired color
- Plastic lawn and garden bags: 2 black
- Size K/10½/6.5mm crochet hook or size needed to obtain gauge
- Tapestry needle
- Black sewing thread
- 1-inch diameter flat black button
- Craft glue or hot glue gun
- Stitch marker

## GAUGE

3 sc = 1 inch; 3 sc rows = 1 inch

## PATTERN NOTES

Read General Instructions before beginning pattern.

Do not join or turn rounds unless otherwise stated. Mark first stitch of each round.

## INSTRUCTIONS

### BAG

**Rnd 1:** With shopping bag strip, ch 9, 3 sc in 2nd ch from hook, sc in each of next 6 chs, 3 sc in last ch, working on opposite side of starting ch, sc in each of next 6 chs. *(18 sc)*

**Rnd 2:** 2 sc in each of first 3 sts, sc in each of next 6 sts, 2 sc in each of next 3 sts, sc in each of last 6 sts, join in beg sc. *(24 sc)*

**Rnd 3:** *[2 sc in next st, sc in next st] 3 times, sc in each of next 6 sts, rep from * once. *(30 sc)*

**Rnd 4:** *[2 sc in next st, sc in each of next 2 sts] 3 times, sc in each of next 6 sts, rep from * once. *(36 sc)*

**Rnd 5:** [Sc in each of next 3 sts, 2 sc in next st] 3 times, sc in each of next 9 sts, [2 sc in next st, sc in each of next 3 sts] 3 times, sc in each of last 3 sts. *(42 sc)*

**Rnd 6:** *[2 sc in next st, sc in each of next 4 sts] 3 times, sc in each of next 6 sts, rep from * once. *(48 sc)*

**Rnd 7:** [Sc in each of next 5 sts, 2 sc in next st] 3 times, sc in each of next 11 sts, [2 sc in next st, sc in each of next 5 sts] 3 times, sc in last st. *(54 sc)*

**Rnd 8:** *[2 sc in next st, sc in each of next 6 sts] 3 times, sc in each of next 6 sts, rep from * once. *(60 sc)*

**Rnd 9:** Working this rnd in **back lps** *(see Stitch Guide) only,* sc in each st around.

**Rnds 10–24:** Sc in each st around.

**Rnd 25:** Sc in each st around, join with sl st in beg sc. Fasten off.

## BUTTONHOLE STRAP

**Row 1:** Working in center 8 sts on 1 side of Bag, join shopping bag strip with sc in first of 8 sts, sc in each of next 7 sts, turn. *(8 sc)*

**Rows 2–13:** Ch 1, sc in each st across, turn.

**Row 14:** Ch 1, sc in each of first 2 sts, for **buttonhole**, ch 4, sk next 4 sts, sc in each of last 2 sts, turn. *(4 sc, 1 ch-4 sp)*

**Row 15:** Ch 1, sc in each st and in each ch across. Fasten off.

## TRIM

Working on last rnd of Bag, join lawn bag strip with sc in first st on right-hand side of Strap, working from left to right, for **reverse sc** *(see Fig. 1),* insert hook in next st to the right, yo, pull lp through, complete as sc, reverse sc in each st across to opposite side of Strap. Fasten off.

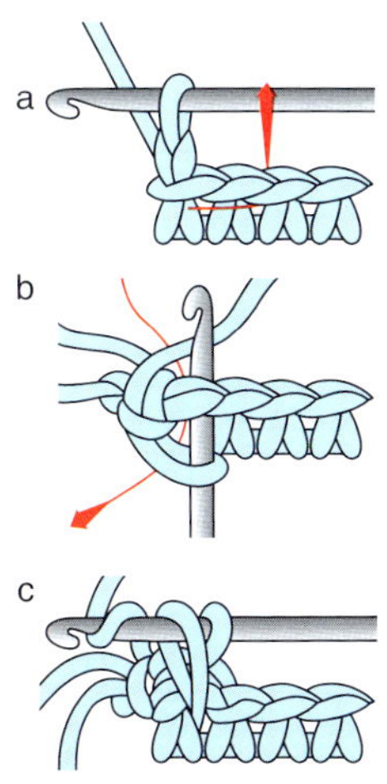


**Fig. 1**
Reverse Single Crochet

Pull Strap over to front side of Bag and sew button to Bag corresponding to buttonhole.

## STRAP

**Row 1:** With lawn bag strip, ch 5, sc in 2nd ch from hook and in each ch across, turn. *(4 sc)*

**Row 2:** Ch 1, sc in each st across, turn.

**Next rows:** Rep row 2 to desired length. Fasten off at end of last row.

Sew 1 end of Strap to each side of Bag.

## ROSE

**Rnd 1:** With lawn bag strip, ch 4, sl st in first ch to form ring, for **petals**, (sc, 3 hdc) 4 times in ring. *(4 petals)*

**Rnd 2:** Sl st around post of first sc, ch 4, [sl st around post of next sc, ch 4] around, join with sl st in beg sl st. *(4 ch sps)*

**Rnd 3:** Ch 1, [sc, hdc, dc, hdc, sc] in each ch sp around, join with sl st in beg sc. *(4 petals)*

**Rnd 4:** Sl st around post of first sc, ch 4, [sl st around post of first sc of next petal, ch 4] around, join with sl in beg sl st. *(4 ch sps)*

**Rnd 5:** Ch 1, (sc, hdc, 2 dc, hdc sc) in each ch sp around, join with sl st in beg sc. *(4 petals)*

**Rnd 6:** Sl st around post of first sc, ch 5, [sl st around post of first sc of next petal, ch 5] around, join with sl st in beg sl st. *(4 ch sps)*

**Rnd 7:** Ch 1, (sc, dc, 2 tr, dc, sc) in each ch sp around, join with sl st in beg sc. Fasten off.

Sew Rose to Buttonhole Tab above buttonhole. ■

# Mini BAG

### SKILL LEVEL

EASY

### FINISHED SIZE

3 x 5 inches, not including Strap

### MATERIALS

- Plastic lawn and garden bags: 2 black
- Size K/10½/6.5mm crochet hook or size needed to obtain gauge
- Tapestry needle
- Black sewing thread
- 1-inch button
- 1 yd pre-strung beads
- Embellishments of choice

### GAUGE

5 sc = 2 inches; 3 sc rows = 1 inch

### PATTERN NOTE

Read General Instructions before beginning pattern.

### INSTRUCTIONS

#### BAG

**Row 1:** Ch 9, sc in 2nd ch from hook and in each ch across, turn. *(8 sc)*

**Rows 2–25:** Ch 1, sc in each st across, turn.

**Row 26:** Ch 1, sc in each of first 2 sts, for **buttonhole**, ch 3, sk next 4 sts, sc in each of last 2 sts, turn. *(4 sc, 1 ch sp)*

**Row 27:** Ch 1, sc in each of first 2 sts, 4 sc in next ch sp, sc in each of last 2 sts. Fasten off.

#### FINISHING

1. Fold first 9 rows up for front and sew ends of rows to corresponding 9 rows on back.

2. Fold rem rows down over front and sew button to Bag corresponding to buttonhole.

3. Using pre-strung beads, attach each end of strand to each side of top of bag to form a strap *(see photo)*.

4. Embellish as desired. ■

# Classic **Hat**

## SKILL LEVEL

EASY

## FINISHED SIZE

Fits 22-inch circumference head

## MATERIALS

- Plastic lawn & garden bags: 14 black
- Size K/10½/6.5mm crochet hook or size needed to obtain gauge
- Embellishments of choice
- Stitch marker

## GAUGE

3 sc = 1 inch; 5 sc rows = 2 inches

## PATTERN NOTES

Read General Instructions before beginning pattern.

Join with slip stitch as indicated unless otherwise stated.

Chain-3 at beginning of rounds counts as first double crochet unless otherwise stated.

Chain-2 at beginning of rounds counts as first half double crochet unless otherwise stated.

## INSTRUCTIONS

### COVER

**Rnd 1:** Ch 6, sl st in first ch to form ring, **ch 3** *(see Pattern Notes)*, 11 dc in ring, **join** *(see Pattern Notes)* in 3rd ch of beg ch-3. *(12 dc)*

**Rnd 2:** Ch 3, dc in same st, 2 dc in each st around, join in 3rd ch of beg ch-3. *(24 dc)*

**Rnd 3:** Ch 3, dc in same st, dc in next st, [2 dc in next st, dc in next st] around, join in 3rd ch of beg ch-3. *(36 dc)*

**Rnd 4:** Ch 3, dc in same st, [dc in each of next 4 sts, 2 dc in next st] around, join in 3rd ch of beg ch-3. *(44 dc)*

**Rnd 5:** Ch 3, dc in same st, [dc in each of next 4 sts, 2 dc in next st] 8 times, dc in each of next 2 sts, 2 dc in last st, join in 3rd ch of beg ch-3. *(54 dc)*

**Rnd 6: Ch 2** *(see Pattern Notes)*, hdc in each st around, join in 2nd ch of beg ch-2. *(54 hdc)*

**Rnds 7–11:** Ch 1, sc in each st around, join in beg sc. Fasten off. *(54 sc)*

**Rnd 12:** Ch 2, 2 hdc in next st, [hdc in next st, 2 hdc in next st] around, join in 2nd ch of beg ch-2. *(81 sc)*

**Rnd 13:** Ch 2, hdc in each st around, join in 2nd ch of beg ch-2.

**Rnds 14–16:** Ch 3, dc in each st around, join in 3rd ch of beg ch-3. Fasten off at end of last rnd. *(81 dc)*.

Roll last 4 rnds up as shown in photo.

Embellish as desired. ■

# Dangling Paillettes Bag

## SKILL LEVEL

EASY

## FINISHED SIZE

7½ inches deep x 10½ inches wide, not including Strap

## MATERIALS

- Plastic lawn and garden bags:
  Approximately 14 black
  Approximately 7 white
- Size K/10½/6.5mm crochet hook or size needed to obtain gauge
- Tapestry needle
- Black sewing thread
- 1½-inch black button
- Stitch marker

## GAUGE

3 sc = 1 inch; 3 sc rows = 1 inch

## PATTERN NOTES

Read General Instructions before beginning pattern.

Do not join or turn rounds unless otherwise stated. Mark first stitch of each round.

## INSTRUCTIONS

### BAG

**Rnd 1:** With black strip, ch 17, 3 sc in 2nd ch from hook, sc in each of next 14 chs, 3 sc in last ch, working on opposite side of starting ch, sc in each of next 17 chs. *(34 sc)*

**Rnd 2:** 2 sc in each of first 3 sts, sc in each of next 14 sts, 2 sc in each of next 3 sts, sc in each of last 14 sts, join in beg sc. *(40 sc)*

**Rnd 3:** *[2 sc in next st, sc in next st] 3 times, sc in each of next 14 sts, rep from * once. *(46 sc)*

**Rnd 4:** *[2 sc in next st, sc in each of next 2 sts] 3 times, sc in each of next 14 sts, rep from * once. *(52 sc)*

**Rnd 5:** [Sc in each of next 3 sts, 2 sc in next st] 3 times, sc in each of next 17 sts, [2 sc in next st, sc in each of next 3 sts] 3 times, sc in each of last 11 sts. *(58 sc)*

**Rnd 6:** *[2 sc in next st, sc in each of next 4 sts] 3 times, sc in each of next 14 sts, rep from * once. *(64 sc)*

**Rnd 7:** Working this rnd in **back lps** *(see Stitch Guide) only,* sc in each st around.

**Rnds 8–19:** Sc in each st around.

**Rnd 20:** Sc in each st around, join with sl st in beg sc. Fasten off.

**Rnd 21:** Join white strip with sc in first st, sc in each st around.

**Rnds 22–24:** Sc in each st around.

**Rnd 25:** Sc in each st around, join with sl st in beg sc. Fasten off.

**Rnd 26:** Join black strip with sc in first st, sc in each st around, join with sl st in beg sc. Fasten off.

## BUTTONHOLE STRAP

**Row 1:** With black strip, ch 8, sc in 2nd ch from hook and in each ch across, turn. *(7 sc)*

**Rows 2–10:** Ch 1, sc in each st across, turn.

**Row 11:** Ch 1, sc in each of first 2 sts, ch 3, sk next 3 sts, sc in each of last 2 sts. Fasten off.

Sew first row of Strap to center of 1 side for back.

Pull Strap over to front side of Bag and sew button to Bag corresponding with buttonhole.

## STRAP

**Row 1:** With black strip, ch 5, sc in 2nd ch from hook and in each ch across, turn. *(4 sc)*

**Row 2:** Ch 1, sc in each st across, turn.

**Next rows:** Rep row 2 to desired length. Fasten off at end of last row.

Sew 1 end of Strap to each side of Bag.

Embellish as desired. ■

**TOLL-FREE ORDER LINE** or to request a free catalog (800) LV-ANNIE (800) 582-6643
**Customer Service** (800) AT-ANNIE (800) 282-6643, **Fax** (800) 882-6643
Visit AnniesAttic.com



ISBN: 978-1-59635-237-7

Printed in USA

1 2 3 4 5 6 7 8 9

# Stitch Guide

## For more complete information, visit **FreePatterns.com**

### ABBREVIATIONS

| | |
|---|---|
| **beg** | begin/begins/beginning |
| **bpdc** | back post double crochet |
| **bpsc** | back post single crochet |
| **bptr** | back post treble crochet |
| **CC** | contrasting color |
| **ch(s)** | chain(s) |
| **ch-** | refers to chain or space previously made (e.g., ch-1 space) |
| **ch sp(s)** | chain space(s) |
| **cl(s)** | cluster(s) |
| **cm** | centimeter(s) |
| **dc** | double crochet (singular/plural) |
| **dc dec** | double crochet 2 or more stitches together, as indicated |
| **dec** | decrease/decreases/decreasing |
| **dtr** | double treble crochet |
| **ext** | extended |
| **fpdc** | front post double crochet |
| **fpsc** | front post single crochet |
| **fptr** | front post treble crochet |
| **g** | gram(s) |
| **hdc** | half double crochet |
| **hdc dec** | half double crochet 2 or more stitches together, as indicated |
| **inc** | increase/increases/increasing |
| **lp(s)** | loop(s) |
| **MC** | main color |
| **mm** | millimeter(s) |
| **oz** | ounce(s) |
| **pc** | popcorn(s) |
| **rem** | remain/remains/remaining |
| **rep(s)** | repeat(s) |
| **rnd(s)** | round(s) |
| **RS** | right side |
| **sc** | single crochet (singular/plural) |
| **sc dec** | single crochet 2 or more stitches together, as indicated |
| **sk** | skip/skipped/skipping |
| **sl st(s)** | slip stitch(es) |
| **sp(s)** | space(s)/spaced |
| **st(s)** | stitch(es) |
| **tog** | together |
| **tr** | treble crochet |
| **trtr** | triple treble |
| **WS** | wrong side |
| **yd(s)** | yard(s) |
| **yo** | yarn over |

**Chain—ch:** Yo, pull through lp on hook.

**Slip stitch—sl st:** Insert hook in st, pull through both lps on hook.

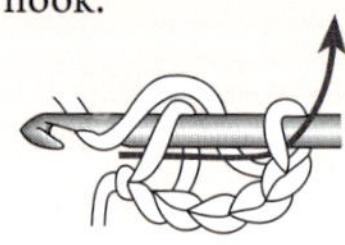

**Single crochet—sc:** Insert hook in st, yo, pull through st, yo, pull through both lps on hook.

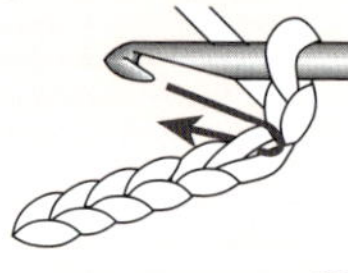

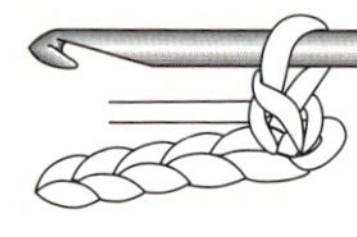

**Front post stitch—fp:** **Back post stitch—bp:** When working post st, insert hook from right to left around post st on previous row.

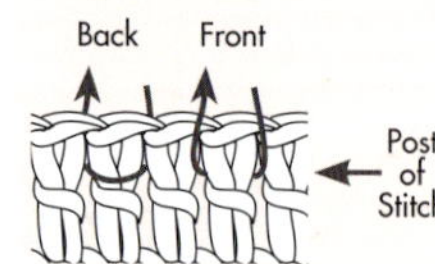


**Front loop—front lp**
**Back loop—back lp**

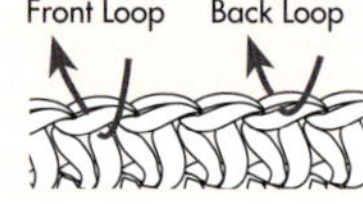


**Half double crochet—hdc:** Yo, insert hook in st, yo, pull through st, yo, pull through all 3 lps on hook.

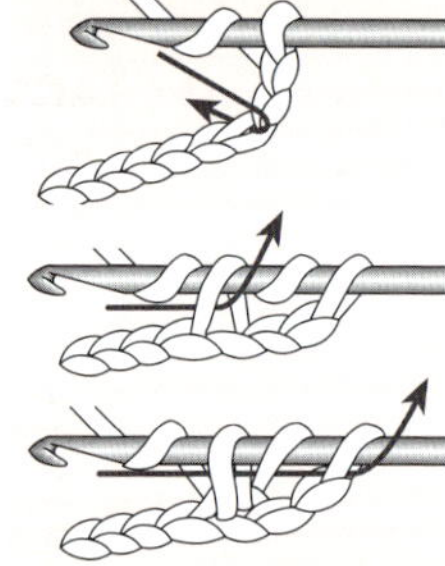

**Double crochet—dc:** Yo, insert hook in st, yo, pull through st, [yo, pull through 2 lps] twice.

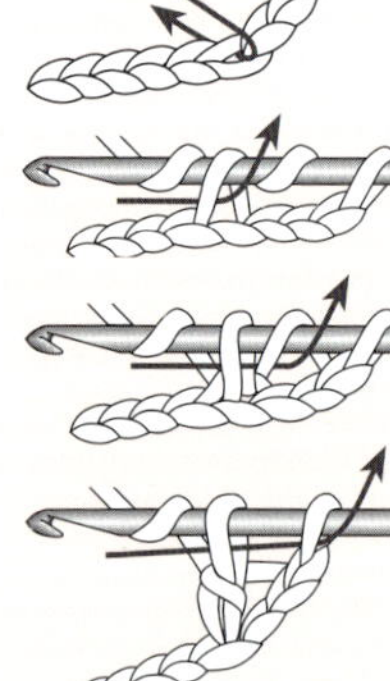

**Change colors:** Drop first color; with 2nd color, pull through last 2 lps of st.

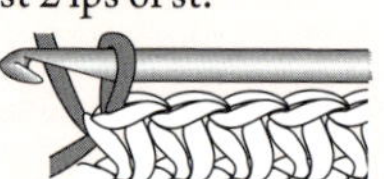

**Treble crochet—tr:** Yo twice, insert hook in st, yo, pull through st, [yo, pull through 2 lps] 3 times.

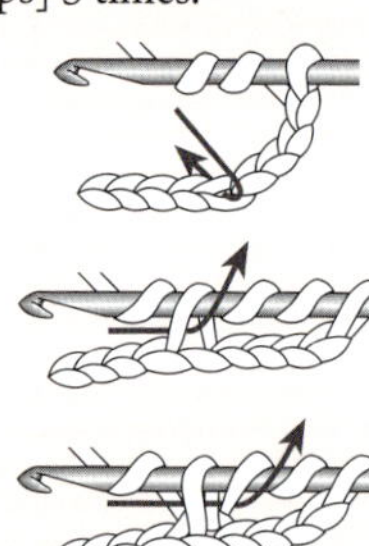

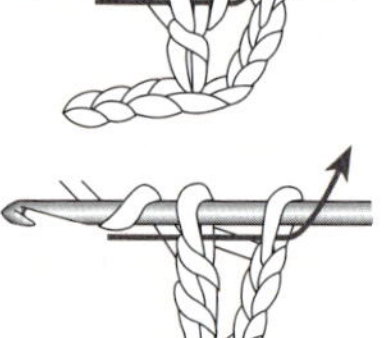

**Double treble crochet—dtr:** Yo 3 times, insert hook in st, yo, pull through st, [yo, pull through 2 lps] 4 times.

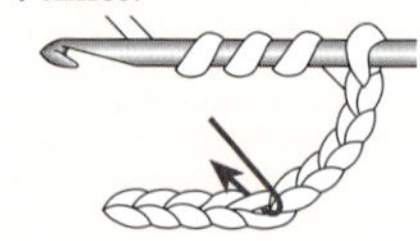

**Single crochet decrease (sc dec):** (Insert hook, yo, draw lp through) in each of the sts indicated, yo, draw through all lps on hook.

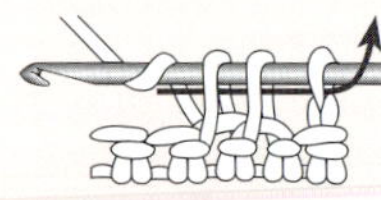

Example of 2-sc dec

**Half double crochet decrease (hdc dec):** (Yo, insert hook, yo, draw lp through) in each of the sts indicated, yo, draw through all lps on hook.

Example of 2-hdc dec

**Double crochet decrease (dc dec):** (Yo, insert hook, yo, draw loop through, draw through 2 lps on hook) in each of the sts indicated, yo, draw through all lps on hook.

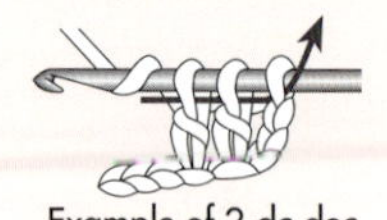

Example of 2-dc dec

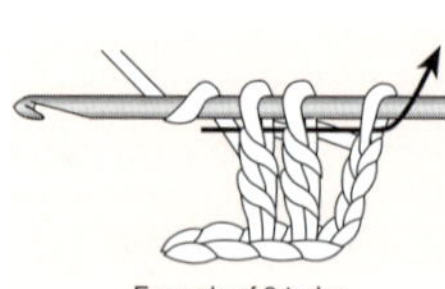

Example of 2-tr dec

**Treble crochet decrease (tr dec):** Holding back last lp of each st, tr in each of the sts indicated, yo, pull through all lps on hook.

| US | | UK |
|---|---|---|
| sl st (slip stitch) | = | sc (single crochet) |
| sc (single crochet) | = | dc (double crochet) |
| hdc (half double crochet) | = | htr (half treble crochet) |
| dc (double crochet) | = | tr (treble crochet) |
| tr (treble crochet) | = | dtr (double treble crochet) |
| dtr (double treble crochet) | = | ttr (triple treble crochet) |
| skip | = | miss |